BEFORE YOU ADOPT

A GUIDE TO THE QUESTIONS YOU SHOULD BE ASKING

A WORKBOOK BY

CHRISTA JORDAN

[Word.robe] Media

2018

BEFORE YOU ADOPT

A Guide To The Questions You Should Be Asking

A Spoonful of Jordan Resource

Nonfiction > Family & Relationships > Adoption & Fostering

Second print edition (white interior), December 2018
Published via Kindle Direct Publishing

ISBN: 9781792898280

Learn more at Christa's blog:
spoonfulofjordan.com

Editing, cover design & layout by Jonathan Jordan / [Word.robe] Media

www.wordrobemedia.com

ACKNOWLEDGMENTS

To my husband/editor: Thank you for cheering me on, for speaking life in the times I was discouraged, felt I couldn't do this or when I was believing lies that I wasn't good enough to take on such a project. You were quick to drown out the nonsense when I wasn't strong enough to. Thank you for being the most patient man to the world's most passionate, Type A woman. I love you and love doing this life alongside you.

To Kai: Thanks, buddy, for being so understanding, for being patient in all the times Mommy was stressed out, and giving me grace. You are my biggest inspiration. You are the most determined person I know, and you never let fear stop you. You teach me to put my fears aside and just go for it, always encouraging me even when you don't understand what it is I'm doing. Being your mom is the absolute best, greatest job that brings me joy every single day. I love you to Neverland and back!

A huge debt of gratitude to all who reviewed my book to give their feedback, correction, and support. Elena Hall (author of *Through Adopted Eyes),* Sarah Damoff (CASA volunteer), Karen McCommas (adoptive and foster mom), Michelle Hurt (soon-to-be adoptive mom and ministry leader), Jill Cucullu & Celeste Liversidge (AdoptMatch), Lanaya Graham (adoptive mom), and Ashley Mitchell (Lifetime Healing LLC). I am incredibly thankful for every one of your perspectives and the time you took to ensure this book was accurate, thorough, and honoring to all members of the adoption triad.

Thank you Cristina Howell, for sharing the gift of your time, knowledge and experience with embryo adoption. Without your help, that section of this book would not be the same. Thank you, friend, for your continued support and encouragement.

To my parents: You have said for years that I should write a book. I finally took your advice and did it! Thank you for always encouraging me to use my strengths, believing in me, encouraging me to get after my goals, and being my biggest, lifetime supporters. I love you guys.

To every one of you who told me to keep going, that this resource was needed and I had to put it out there, thank you for speaking life into me.

CONTENTS

FOREWORD

Adoption is hard. And beautiful. And kind of a mystery, even for those who have walked through it before. My lovely wife and I had a lot of personal experience in social work and the world of adoption before we even began our first adoption journey, and yet it was amazing how much we learned just through the process ourselves - and how much we are *still* learning now as parents.

Even as adoption advocates, we have found that we have had to change our own way of thinking about adoption. It's not a one-off event - "There! Done! Success!" Rather, adoption is a lifelong commitment. It is an ongoing conversation, and each conversation is just as unique as the DNA that makes each of us an individual.

This workbook was born out of a lot of conversations and tears and hard days. Anyone who knows my wife knows that she excels at many things, but one of those is her uncanny gift to ask intentional and thoughtful questions.

The questions in here are designed to make you think - *hard*. They are not simple "yes" or "no" questions because life is more complicated than that. And whether or not you adopt - and *how*, and *where from*, and *who* - deserves a lot of thought and attention.

I may be completely and utterly biased by the fact that she is my wife, but I think this book is incredibly insightful and invaluable for those who are beginning their adoption journey. Or maybe you've adopted before and want to keep from repeating some mistakes. We've been there, too, trust me.

Whatever the case and whatever circumstance brought you to adoption, we're in this together. There's no judgment here, no condemnation - just helpful thoughts and a hope that we can grow together.

Don't expect to be done with this in a day. And even if you *think* you already know which route of adoption you're going to take, I'd urge you to go through *all* the sections and *all* the questions. You may surprise yourself, and you may discover that a question in one section helps you better process another question elsewhere.

That being said, I'm going to get out of the way now. But not before leaving you with one question of my own: *What are you waiting for?*

Jonathan Jordan
husband, father, storyteller, editor, and maker of nachos

INTRODUCTION

Friend, I am so glad to meet you here. Here in this place where you are contemplating adoption. Maybe this is something that has been on your heart and mind for years, maybe this is something you just recently started to consider. Maybe you've been walking the incredibly difficult road of infertility, maybe you are just starting to consider different ways to grow your family. Maybe you're married, maybe you're single. Whatever road and season you are in right now, this was made to meet you right where you are.

I know that this journey (and *all* the things that come with it) can be overwhelming. Search the word *adoption* or *foster care* online and you'll get lost in the internet for days. Because we are all in different seasons and paths, we are going to be called and moved to different things, and that's *good*. Sometimes, though, we need a little guidance. We need to ask good questions to get to the heart of the matter. We need to take the grand vision and break it down into smaller parts to help us *digest* and *decide*. That's why I wanted to create this resource, so you can best figure out which path is right for you, your family, and your current season.

This is not the "end all, be all" resource. I believe you should always be learning and growing - that never stops. But this is a good starting place. This workbook asks a lot of questions; some are easy, many will make you think and dig deeper. If you become overwhelmed, take a deep breath and come back, because I promise that we will untangle things together. There's also an intentional blank space at the end of the book to right down anything you need to further process, discuss, or find more answers. And, as an adoptive parent, I wish I would have had something like this before we started this journey, for someone to ask *me* the hard questions I wasn't thinking about, because you don't know what you don't know.

Before you even begin to choose the type of adoption, find an agency, and start printing out all the paperwork, *long* before you bring your child or children into your family, I want you to be as well-equipped and well-prepared as possible. I don't want you fumbling through parenting and juggling a million things and tasks while also trying to deal with really heavy situations you never thought of or discussed. If you're married, I want you and your spouse to be 100% on the same page before you begin anything, and if you're single I want to make sure you've got a tribe in your corner ready to support you for the long haul in the right ways. Whether it's my health or my parenting, I'm always about being on the preventative side of things, not waiting for disaster to strike before I make a plan. All of these things are real and important, and I'm asking them because my family has experienced this ourselves, or walked with people who have, and I believe we will see healthier, thriving families if we simply do some (deep) work on the front end of things.

This resource and guide is meant to narrow down the bigness of adoption, make it smaller and have all your thoughts in one place. This is meant to be done individually, but also in community. If you are married, you should *each* have a workbook that you are answering these questions separately, then coming together to discuss them. If you are single, ask the closest person you know who will be in your corner to listen to your heart as you process these things. Married or single, find others already walking this road. Get around them, process some of these things with them. Ask them hard questions and listen to their answers.

Know this: adoption is a journey. The work will continue in different ways and different seasons, but I hope that this starting point will also give you a framework to ask yourself the hard questions as you hit those times. Because you *will* hit those times, I promise.

I'll be here, cheering you on, pouring you extra coffee and praying you through this thing.

Until there is more than enough,

Christa

STEPS

These are the steps my husband and I walk people through when they want to pursue adoption but feel overwhelmed and unsure where to start. Many times, people are all over the map and want to start looking at agencies before they even know what type of adoption they should pursue.

You don't *have* to go in this order, but we believe this makes things easier, smoother, and provides a much clearer path and more natural rhythm overall. Decisions regarding adoption and foster care aren't something you should ever rush through. I know you may be excited, passionate, and ready, but you need to make sure this is done *right* and with wisdom and care.

1. **Explore the types of adoption**, and decide which type is the best fit for your family, in your current season.

2. **Explore different agencies**, and pick the best fit for your family.

3. **Start the paperwork**.

ADDRESSING EXPECTATIONS

We all come to adoption for different reasons, in different ways, and different seasons. Like every parent, there are hopes and dreams and things you envision for your family, but adoption and foster care bring up unique situations and motivations for growing your family.

Whatever route you take, it's important to remember that you will not be your child's first chapter in their family history. Even if you are the legal guardian of your child(ren) from the moment of birth, there is no such thing as a "blank slate."

You may not have had a chance yet to even think about your expectations because they are so automatic and deeply-rooted. These are not easy questions. These are questions that are going to make you dig very deep, because our hope is to help prevent damage done when these issues are not addressed beforehand. The desire here is to have healthy, thriving families, and part of that is discovering what is underneath the surface in yourself before bringing your child(ren) home.

QUESTIONS ABOUT YOUR EXPECTATIONS

1. What is your main - or most immediate - motivation for adopting?

2. What are some areas of your life where you are feeling unsatisfied or lacking?

3. Are there unresolved issues/pain from past relationships and/or infertility issues that need to be addressed *before* you begin this process?

4. What are your fears, hesitations, "worst case scenarios" you have about adoption/ foster care?

5. Are those things true, myths, or hearsay? How did you come to believe those things?

6. Do you know anyone who has walked this road and can speak to those issues?

7. Do you feel any shame in growing your family through adoption?

8. Why are you considering adoption as an option to grow your family?

9. How would you define discipline?

10. How were you disciplined as a child?

11. Would you implement those same strategies with your children? Is there anything you would change?

12. What do you know about trauma, the brain, and how it effects attachment?

13. In what ways might foster care or adoption require you to parent differently than how you were parented or how your community parents? If you have children already in your home, are there ways your discipline methods would need to change?

14. What are ways that you can explore your own childhood, the good and the bad, and how those things can affect your parenting now?

15. What is your biggest concern parenting a child who does not share your DNA (i.e. your looks, health history, attributes, mannerisms)?

16. Do you have any plans to pursue pregnancy while also pursuing adoption? If yes, and you do become pregnant during the adoption process, how will you move forward?

17. Is there anything about your current financial status that you believe is hindering you from moving forward with adoption or a specific type of adoption?

18. Can you think of creative ways to raise support for adoption that go well with you and your spouse's personalities, lifestyle, and interests?

19. What does your extended family know about adoption?

20. Do you believe they will have any concerns? How will you educate them along the way?

21. How will you share your journey with others, but also protect your child's story, especially on social media?

22. What makes you most excited when you think about building your family through adoption?

GENERAL QUESTIONS ABOUT ADOPTION

No matter what type of adoption you choose, there are general things to consider regarding any kind of adoption: resources that may be available to you, things that you need to know and decide regarding your current family structure and how to best move forward.

It is important to lay a solid foundation, and build upon that foundation as you continue to learn, discuss, and answer things honestly. These types of general adoption questions lay the groundwork, so take your time and don't rush through, as the answer to these will better inform you to discern what is best as you explore the different types of adoption.

1. Do you have a good support system around you? Are there family and loyal friends close by who will help you through the process?

2. Do you have access to trauma-informed babysitters/respite care providers? If not, who would you ask to be trained as a trauma-informed care provider?

3. Does your current job allow for "maternity/paternity leave" for adoption/foster care placements?

4. Does your current job give any financial assistance/incentive for adoption and/or daycare options?

5. Does your health insurance plan or alternative healthcare provider offer any financial assistance/incentive for adoption?

6. What age range(s) are you open to? What is your reasoning behind this or specific need for that age range?

7. If you have children in your home, have you asked them about their feelings surrounding foster care and/or adoption? Have you let them voice their concerns or questions yet?

8. Children already in your home and their current ages:

9. Are you open to sibling groups?

10. What do you know about adopting out of birth order? Is this something you would be willing to do? For example, if you have biological children, would you adopt children who are their same age or older than they are? How would you help your children transition into a new role of being the younger sibling(s), etc.?

11. Personal history of children in your home (medical or behavioral issues, adopted or biological):

12. Special needs currently present in your home (medical, behavioral, allergies, etc.):

13. Are you open to parenting a child with any minor or major medical needs? If so, what level of needs do you feel like your family could handle?

14. What type of therapies does your insurance provider cover (counseling, play therapy, occupational therapy, speech therapy, physical therapy, etc.)? If your insurance does not cover a type of therapy or only a certain amount of sessions that your child would need, how would you cover the rest?

Note: If you do foster-to-adopt in the US, foster children are insured through the Medicaid program of your state, and those types of therapies should be covered.

15. Would a particular type of adoption trigger any issues with the children currently in your home?

16. In every type of adoption, you will be dealing with lots of different legal paperwork and documentation. What are some ways that you will keep up with everything - for example, due dates, documentation, etc.? What are some practical tools you have available to help you be organized?

17. Does your current community include other foster or adoptive families? How do you think that will affect your foster or adoptive children?

BECOMING A MULTICULTURAL FAMILY

It is very common for families to adopt or foster outside of their race, ethnicity and culture. DNA does not make a family, but you must explore and consider the effect this will have on your child and family.

No matter what route of adoption you take, your family will become multicultural to some degree. Depending on your situation, this could mean adding children to your family from another racial group, mixed-racial group, nationality, different socioeconomic class, different geographic region, and language.

These questions are designed make you think about those potential issues, expose things that may need to be exposed, and help you to begin to do some work to be prepare yourself, your current child(ren), and your future child(ren) for the cultural challenges you will face together.

1. What is your personal experience with racism?

2. What is your response when you see racism? How do you currently fight against it?

3. Are you willing to parent a child outside of your race, ethnicity and culture?

4. If so, how will you teach your child and incorporate their birth culture as much as possible?

5. What does your current neighborhood, friendship circles, families around you, your own family, church community, school, etc. look like? Is it highly diverse or does everyone look the same? What are ways you might need to diversify your current lifestyle, and are you willing to do that?

6. Will you be able to parent a child outside of your race, ethnicity, and culture well? What steps will you take to ensure your child is getting what he/she needs?

7. Do you already have people around you *now* who look different from you, or will your child be the only one? If yes, how do you think this will affect them long-term?

8. Is there anyone in your extended family or friendships that you would worry about their support, especially if it is a child outside of your race, ethnicity and culture? How will you address this?

EXPLORING THE TYPES OF ADOPTION

FOSTER CARE & FOSTER-TO-ADOPT

In the US, the term *foster care* generally refers to the system and process in which minor children are removed from their home by a government agency due to physical abuse, sexual abuse, emotional abuse, medical abuse, or severe neglect.

If there are relatives willing and able to take the child(ren), and they can clear the necessary government-mandated requirements, the child(ren) will likely be placed with the family first.

If that is not an option, they are placed with a foster parent who is licensed through the state, or a facility licensed for foster care, such as a group home or residential treatment center.

The intended goal of foster care is family reunification, the restoration of the family unit. Therefore, some foster parents *only* foster, meaning they are not looking to adopt, but care for the child(ren) until reunification can occur or a permanent placement elsewhere happens.

Others choose to *foster-to-adopt*, meaning they are willing to become the permanent family if reunification is not an option and no kinship placement is available. It is important to note here that all possibilities of kinship placement will be exhausted first before the foster-to-adopt family will be considered to be the permanent family.

One can also choose to be licensed to *adopt only* from the foster care system. This means the adoptive parents will only accept placement of a *waiting child*. In the foster care system, waiting children are those whose parents' parental rights have already been terminated or relinquished, and therefore they are legally free to be adopted.

QUESTIONS TO ASK BEFORE PURSUING FOSTER CARE

1. What do you know about the foster care system in your state?

2. What do you believe about children in foster care?

3. Why do you think so many children <u>age out</u> of the system? (Age out: child becomes a legal adult without being adopted or reunified with family.)

4. What behavioral issues are you concerned about with parenting kids who have endured abuse and neglect?

5. What do you believe about the biological parents of kids in foster care?

6. What are your initial thoughts about the concept of family reunification?

7. What do you believe is <u>your</u> role in supporting the reunification process and the parents?

8. How will you speak about the biological parents to the child(ren) in your care?

9. What fears and hesitations do you have about bringing children into your home that you know might not stay forever?

10. What do you believe children in foster care need the most?

11. If you currently have children, what concerns do you have about how they will handle having children in the home who may stay only for a season?

12. If you currently have children, how will you communicate and explain foster care to them?

13. If you are married, does one of you have a flexible schedule to be able to transport children in your care and attend all the necessary appointments, visits, and meetings required?

14. If you are single, will your current employer be understanding and accommodating when appointments, visits, court dates, etc. come up?

15. What would be your plan for sudden child placements (i.e. emergency placement at 2 am), or for a sudden child discharge (i.e. child services has been ordered to immediately release child to new guardian/relative)?

16. Are there currently any support groups that you know of in your area for foster parents?

17. What kinds of support do you believe you will need when you first receive a placement and throughout your journey?

18. Who are the people in your life that you know will make a good support team?

19. If you are fostering a child and find out there is another sibling, older or younger, would you be willing to also foster the sibling(s)? If they are already adopted, would you be willing to have a connection with their adoptive family to keep the siblings connected?

20. If there are biological family members willing to maintain a connection, what type of contact would you be willing to keep with them?

With foster care, you are parenting a child who is not legally your child until an adoption is finalized, so there are many rules regarding where you can take this child and with whom you may trust to their care in your absence. For instance, you cannot just call up a neighbor if you need to run to the store or hire the teenager next door for a date night. All babysitters and caregivers must have a background check and be CPR/First Aid certified, at minimum.

Depending on the case and your agency's requirements, you may need to obtain permission to go out of the county, cross state lines, or even go on extended vacations.

Other times, due to the stress of trauma, you as the caregivers may just need a break and recharge with some self care, whether this be a date night or weekend getaway. In those cases, you will need to request respite care.

21. If you have a vacation planned or an event to go to at the time you receive a new child into your home, how will you handle that situation? What protocols should you set in place to be prepared for this situation?

22. Is there anyone close to you who would be willing and able to become certified for respite care?

23. Is there anyone you currently know who has experience with foster care (professionally, volunteering, or parent) that you could talk to?

24. What are some other ways that you can currently serve in foster care to gain experience?

25. What is you main motivation for considering this type of adoption?

PRIVATE DOMESTIC ADOPTION

A *private domestic adoption* happens when a woman who faces an unplanned pregnancy chooses to place her child for adoption. Prospective adoptive parents choose an agency and complete all the necessary legal requirements, such as a home study, background checks, classes.

Typically, prospective adoptive parents put together a profile book or create an electronic profile for expectant mothers to review. When an expectant mother chooses a family for her child, the agency facilitates the next steps and conversations between the expectant mother and prospective adoptive parents.

In certain situations, instead of an agency, just an adoption attorney may be involved in the process by negotiating the terms of adoption between the prospective adoptive parents and the expectant mother.

It is becoming more common for agencies and attorneys to expect prospective adoptive parents to self-match. This means that they independently use a service to match with an expectant mother after they have been licensed to adopt through an agency. After being chosen by the expectant mother, an agreement is created according to the agency's policies and process, and the adoption attorney assists in negotiating the terms of the adoption. It is important for the expectant mother and the adoptive parents to have *separate* legal representation when negotiating the terms of adoption.

Concerning *adoption facilitators* and *adoption consultants*, an extra measure of caution and research should be undertaken by prospective adoptive parents. Adoption facilitators are technically illegal in most states but still find ways to advertise their services. They charge flat fees to assist in matching, but may engage in unethical or questionable methods, such as financial coercion of a birth mother, or taking advantage of pregnant women in dire situations. Adoption consultants are often unlicensed individuals that offer support services, such as assisting a family in creating their profile or advising a family through the process. While not all bad, be wary of those that claim to help families find matches.

Private domestic adoptions may include *closed*, *open*, or *semi-open* adoptions depending on the wishes of the birth mother and agreement with the adoptive family.

Closed Adoption: After expectant mother relinquishes her parental rights and child is adopted, there is no contact between birth mother and adoptive parents and child.

Semi-Open Adoption: Expectant mother relinquishes her rights, and adoptive parent sends a set amount of pictures, letters, updates, may have a few phone calls or one visit per year. This is typically done through the agency so there is not much direct contact between birth mother, adoptive parents, and child.

Open Adoption: Expectant mother relinquishes her rights, but makes a plan with adoptive parents and continues contact and relationship between birth mother, adoptive parents, and child. This relationship looks different for each family and often changes over time.

It is important to note that in legal terms, the adoptive parents are not considered the lawful parents until the expectant mother and biological father have relinquished their parental rights. After the child is born, the law can vary from state to state, but typically there is a forty-eight to seventy-two hour wait time in which the biological mother can voluntarily terminate her rights. During this time, she is still legally the child's mother and may freely decide to parent, even if an adoption plan has been made. Depending upon the laws of the state of residence, a mother's consent is generally irrevocable anywhere from one to thirty days after executing the relinquishment.

You can adopt outside of your state, and in such cases, the adoptive parents will be required to travel to their child's birth state and must wait for clearance to return home with their child. This clearance is known as "ICPC" which stands for Interstate Compact on the Placement of Children. This ensures the legal transport of children across state lines and once all paperwork is complete and approved in both the child's birth state and the adoptive parent's home state, then the family will be released to travel back home. ICPC time can vary, but typically occurs between three to ten business days.

QUESTIONS TO ASK BEFORE PURSUING PRIVATE DOMESTIC ADOPTION

1. What do you know about private domestic adoption?

2. What types of services do you believe the expectant mothers should receive?

3. What do you believe about women who place their child for adoption? What do you think are some of the circumstances that might bring them to that decision?

4. What types of financial assistance do you believe the adoptive parents should be responsible for with the expectant mother?

5. What rights do you believe the expectant mother has during pregnancy, labor, and delivery?

6. What rights do you believe the adoptive parent/parents have during pregnancy, labor, and delivery?

7. What is your hope for a potential birth mom's future beyond the birth and adoption?

8. What are some ways that you can support the birth mom and have an ongoing relationship with her, if possible? What would that ideally look like for your family?

9. What are your initial thoughts on closed, semi-open, or open adoption? Why?

Closed Adoption

Semi-Open Adoption

Open Adoption:

10. What are your fears and hesitations with an open adoption?

11. Are you willing to stay connected to your child's birth mother (and potentially other members from the birth family)? Why or why not?

12. What would keep you from having an open adoption?

13. Do you feel like there is a competition between birth mom and adoptive mom? How will you handle those feelings if they arise?

14. What do you believe is the responsibility of the adoption agency to the expectant mom?

15. What do you believe is the responsibility of the adoption agency to the adoptive parents?

16. If you are chosen by an expectant mother, and then she decides to parent, how would you handle that? Would that change your view of her? Would you commit to supporting her in that decision, and what would that look like?

17. What kinds of post-adoption services and support do you believe the birth mom should receive?

18. What kinds of post-adoption services and support do you believe should be available for the adoptive parents?

19. Do you believe that adopting at birth brings about the same effects of trauma as other types of adoption? Why or why not?

20. How will you speak to your child about his/her birth family?

21. How will you help your child process his/her adoption story?

22. What will you do if, due to her own grief and trauma, your child's birth mother stops responding? How will you support her? How will you explain this to your child? Should she begin to respond again, how will you respond to her?

23. Is cost something that would initially dissuade you from this type of adoption? Do you have any experience with fundraising?

24. Do you currently know anyone who has experience with this type of adoption (birth mother, adoptive parent, adoptee, professional) that you could talk to?

25. What are ways that you can currently serve women in crisis and empower them to parent if they choose to keep their child?

26. What is your main motivation for considering this type of adoption?

INTERNATIONAL ADOPTION

International adoption is when parents adopt a child or children who live in another country outside of the one in which they are a citizen. Adoptive parents work with an agency in their home country who has a partnership program in the birth country of their child.

Prospective parents must meet all the legal requirements laid out by both the birth country and their home country, and there must be legal documentation to show that the birth parents' parental rights have been relinquished or there is a qualifying case for abandonment. These qualifications will vary from country to country.

Parents must also be prepared to walk through the immigration and citizenship process required by their country and must also be ready to comply with the birth country's protocol, including any requirements to possibly travel multiple times and/or reside within the birth country for a set period of time. Internationally-adopted children may also continue to have birthrights to their country of origin, such as dual citizenship. If this is the case, be familiar with how citizenship and adoption laws change as the child grows up, and how this could affect future travel to the child's country of origin.

Hague Treaty: An agreement between countries intended to set standards for ethical practices among countries for international adoptions. The full effect of the convention began in 2008, and countries may continue to become part of the Hague as they choose. You can adopt from countries *not* a part of the Hague, but the process looks different.

The most reliable, comprehensive source for this in the United States is the Department of State website. This site will give you updates on what is going on with each country, whether or not they are a part of the Hague, and an overview of the country's process and requirements so you can best see how to move forward.

Because each country has different laws and requirements surrounding adoption, it is highly recommended to first narrow your options to two or three countries that you would like to adopt from. Otherwise, it can be overwhelming as you search all the different requirements. A smaller list of countries will also help you narrow down which agency to choose, as certain agencies only work with certain countries where they have established programs.

QUESTIONS TO ASK BEFORE PURSUING INTERNATIONAL ADOPTION

1. What do you know about international adoption?

2. Is there a connection that you have to a particular country and/or culture?

3. Why do you believe children end up in institutions like orphanages?

4. What kinds of things would a child in an orphanage be missing out on? How do you think this impacts them long-term?

5. What are some of the challenges you think you might face with this type of adoption?

6. How do you feel about parenting a child with little to no knowledge of their birth history?

7. What age range of children do you think would be a good fit in your home? Are children of this age range released for adoption in the countries you are considering?

8. What level of medical needs do you believe your family could handle?

9. Because the child is not getting the same type of care they would in a family setting, it is highly likely there will be developmental delays, especially due to trauma. Sometimes these things can go misdiagnosed, and you may not have full answers until after you arrive back home. If this is the case, how will you handle a misdiagnosis, for better or worse?

10. How will you help your child "catch up" on developmental delays? For example, is there a network of therapists or programs in your area?

11. Outside of your parenting, what are some ways you could advocate for your child to get the help they need? For example, if you experience indifference or insensitivity from a teacher or other authority figure?

12. What fears or hesitations do you have about adopting a child from another country?

13. What are some ways that you would incorporate your child's birth country and culture into your family?

14. If you do not come from the same culture/ethnicity as your child, how do you plan to teach them about where they are from?

15. How will you address questions about birth family/history from your child?

16. How will you help your child(ren) process their time in an orphanage (or other institution) and what they experienced there?

17. How will you deal with language barriers when first arriving in country and when bringing your child(ren) home?

18. How will you teach your child your language? Will you learn their birth language or help them retain their birth language?

19. How would you help your child adjust to dietary changes? Will you learn to cook dishes from their birth country? What do you know about malnutrition or other feeding problems?

20. Are you open to keeping a connection and relationship with family members in their birth country, if possible?

21. What are your thoughts on helping your child discover information on their birth family/history? Would you consider taking trips to their birth country to help them stay connected to their birthplace and culture?

22. If you do not already have a personal connection to a current country, which countries do you fit the requirements for?

23. If you are in process to adopt from a country, and for whatever reason, that government decides to put adoptions on hold or close the country to adoptions, how would you handle that?

24. Are finances something that would keep you from considering this type of adoption? Do you have any experience with fundraising?

25. Does your current employer offer flexibility with your schedule or PTO plan if you need to stay in country for an extended period of time?

26. If you currently have children, will they travel with you to your child's birth country at the time of placement? Do you have childcare easily available and accessible for an extended period of time?

Many times, there is culture shock for a child of any age. They are in a new home with a new family they don't yet know, a new country where everything is overwhelming: sights, smells, *everything* is different. It may seem like the best thing to do is to "jump into" regular life and routine, but there can be many triggers for your child with that mindset.

After all, *your* sense of normalcy is not *their* experience of normalcy. For example, traditional public school may not be possible at first due to their transitional needs. It is highly recommended to keep a child's world "small" in their first few months home with you. Otherwise, there could be unintentional expectations that set the child up for failure and lead to behavioral or social issues.

27. When you first arrive home with your child, what are some ways that you will help keep your child's world "small" to help them transition into family life and establish a new sense of normalcy?

28. Do you currently know anyone who has experience with this type of adoption (adoptive parent, adoptee, professional) that you could talk to?

29. What are ways that you can currently serve this population and get involved, even from afar?

30. What is your main motivation for considering this type of adoption?

EMBRYO ADOPTION

Embryo adoption occurs after a couple who has undergone in vitro fertilization (IVF) has embryos remaining that they then donate to the adoptive parent(s). When the *genetic family* chooses the *adoptive family*, necessary legal paperwork and home study is completed, and the adoptive family is then legally declared to be the parent(s) of the embryos. The embryos are then transferred to the adoptive mother's uterus, and the adoptive mom carries and delivers the child.

The exact manner of the legal transfer of embryos will depend on whether or not you use an agency, go through a matching site or self-match, but all routes will involve legal documentation and paperwork drawn up by an attorney. Once completed, the holding organization of the embryos may safely ship them to the holding organization of the adoptive parent's choice to make the transfer, or the adoptive parent may travel to the holding site. This will be agreed upon and set in the legal documentation.

This type of adoption is still very new, but the need is growing. It is technically and legally seen as a donation.

QUESTIONS TO ASK BEFORE PURSUING EMBRYO ADOPTION

1. What do you know about embryo adoption?

2. Do you have any experience with IVF (in vitro fertilization)?

3. Do you currently have any known medical issues that would make it difficult to carry a pregnancy to term?

4. Have you ever experienced a miscarriage before? If yes, how did you process your grief? If no, do you know anyone who has walked through it that might be able to provide you some perspective?

5. What are your personal beliefs about when human life begins?

6. Are there currently any fertility issues with you or your spouse?

7. Have you experienced pregnancy before? Were there any complications or cause for concern with future pregnancies?

8. To your knowledge, would it be healthy for you to carry twins or multiples?

9. What are your thoughts on carrying and giving birth to a child or children who are not genetically yours, and will not look like you and your spouse?

10. Are you willing to have a relationship with the genetic parents and siblings?

11. What do you think an ongoing relationship with the genetic family would look like for you and your child(ren)?

12. Because some embryos are frozen for many years, some may not survive during the thawing process. How many embryos would you be willing to adopt? Will you be willing to adopt all of the embryos from a donor family?

13. What is the minimum and maximum number of embryos you would consider adopting?

14. How many embryos would you be willing to transfer at one time?

15. Are you prepared to give birth to multiple children at one time? If you currently have children (or you plan to adopt several embryos) and you end up with a set of multiples after one transfer, what will be your plan for the rest of the embryos?

16. Would you want the embryos genetically tested? What would that mean to you and what would you do with the results?

17. If you currently have children, how would you explain embryo adoption to them?

18. What are your initial concerns with this type of adoption?

19. Do you currently know anyone who has experience with this type of adoption (genetic parent, adoptive parent, adoptee, professional) that you could talk to?

20. What is your main motivation for considering this type of adoption?

FINDING THE RIGHT AGENCY

Many people don't know what to look for when finding agencies, and generally base their decisions on which agencies friends have used or who can process paperwork fastest. While these are not necessarily bad factors to consider, they should not be the primary points to consider when selecting an agency.

It is incredibly crucial that you find 1) an agency who has ethical practices and accreditations, and 2) one that best fits the needs of *your* family. I am often asked for a list of agencies I "approve" of, but the problem is our personalities and needs are different from each other. Just because I like a particular agency doesn't mean you will. Therefore, the foundation should be whether or not an agency is ethical, but the rest is going to be based on what you need and who you best *mesh* with.

After you choose the type of adoption route you will pursue, this section of questions will help narrow down the agencies for you, as not all agencies offer each type of adoption. No matter what type of adoption you pursue, the most important thing you will want to be sure of is that the agency is ethical and has clear guidelines and standards for ethical adoptions, and you will need to ask good questions in order to really know that, and not just what they say on their website.

These questions will lead you through that, but please do not settle for ambiguous answers! For instance, if you ask, "What is your protocol when a woman with an unplanned pregnancy seeks help from your agency?" and their answer is something like, "We make sure she's well-taken care of," that's **not good enough**. Ask them for specific proof, tangible examples, and information about what that looks like and what services they are providing.

This is still a business, and unfortunately there are agencies out there who pocket and profit too much money and treat their clients as a commodity instead of serving them with fundamental rights they have and deserve. There are agencies who prey on ignorance, crisis, and hope, and take advantage of both expectant mothers and potential adoptive parents. I want to make sure you guard yourself from enabling such agencies and that you only work with agencies who are above reproach in their standards and are verifiably ethical in their practices.

Additional Tips to Consider:

1. If you are doing international adoption, you are not limited to local agencies. You can choose *any* agency in the US, which opens up your options. However, your home study will need to be conducted by a licensed agency within your state.

2. Before you start calling agencies, make sure you and your spouse have a list of close-handed things you *both* want (outside of ethics) specific to your family. Are there "must-haves" that you just *will not* compromise on, like scope of support, faith statements, etc.? Discuss and write those down in the back of the workbook on the **Agency Must-Haves** page. (Page 99)

3. As you start calling around, narrow it down to your top three favorite agencies. Then take this "Top 3" list and attend a meeting or webinar for each. The best way to really know whether or not an agency will be a good fit is to attend an in-person informational meeting or an online webinar if they aren't local to you. Write down your Top 3 and the important info on the **Top 3 Agencies** page in the back of the book. (Pages 100-103)

Make sure to have a notebook and pen handy to take notes on the answers and make sure you keep up with it in a safe place! If you're really Type A, you can make some kind of spreadsheet to keep it all together.

GENERAL QUESTIONS TO ASK ANY AGENCY

1. When was your agency founded? By whom? And why was the agency founded?

2. What are your current accreditations?

3. How long have you had those accreditations?

4. What are the professional requirements for your staff (ex: social work degrees, licenses, experience and expertise)?

5. What is the average time staff stays with you, particularly caseworkers? What is your staff turn-over rate?

6. What is the breakdown of fees for "X" type of adoption?
*Note: Make sure this is a **detailed** breakdown. If they cannot tell you where the money goes and how it is being used, that is a red flag.*

7. How many families have you served? Or, how many do you serve in a year?

8. How many families are currently using your services?

9. Have you seen an increase or decrease in number of families?

10. What are the general requirements needed for this agency?

11. What are typical things you look for when working with families?

12. Do you have any webinars or informational meetings coming up?

QUESTIONS TO ASK FOSTER CARE AGENCIES

Note: the term "caseworker" here is meant to generally cover any paid position that works in case management with a child or family. Individual agencies may have a different term, like case manager, care worker, family services worker, etc.

1. How do you assign families to caseworkers? What is it based on?

2. What happens if a caseworker leaves or is dismissed in the middle of a placement?

3. What is the system for tracking and maintaining documentation and paperwork in the office?

4. What types of paperwork and documentations are parents responsible for?

5. What type of support do you offer your foster families (ex: support groups, outings, respite nights, holiday and birthday gift programs, clothing vouchers, etc.)?

6. How do you provide community among the foster families and children within your agency? Is that something that is important to the agency?

7. If there is a problem between a caseworker and family, how is it managed?

8. If a child needs something the family cannot afford and the state cannot provide, how is that need met?

9. What happens if we accept a placement and find that it's not working out or not a good fit for the child or our family? What are the discharge protocols and procedures?

10. How much information do you provide to prospective parents about the child's social and medical history prior to the placement?

11. If we choose to pass on a particular placement request, how will that impact our eligibility for future placements?

QUESTIONS TO ASK PRIVATE DOMESTIC ADOPTION AGENCIES

1. When a woman comes to the agency with an unplanned pregnancy and is looking for help and counsel, what is the agency's protocol? What does the follow-up look like?

2. If the expectant mother decides to place the child for adoption, what are the services she is provided through the agency (ex: support groups, counseling, job training, housing, medical needs)?

3. Is the expectant mother provided with her own lawyer? How is the process explained to her throughout her pregnancy?

4. Do you believe the agency should match the expectant mother with the prospective adoptive family? Do you believe that the expectant mother should choose the family?

5. What happens if an expectant mother chooses our family, but then decides she wants to parent the child? Do you continue to serve and support her or is she expected to pay back any assistance she received? What happens to our profile at that point?

6. What post-adoption support is offered to the expectant mother? For how long may she receive support services?

7. What post-adoption support is the adoptive family offered? For how long?

8. What is your stance on open adoptions? How are they facilitated?

9. Do you offer any kind of support/community for the adopted children, especially as they get older?

10. What types of training and educational materials are required for prospective adoptive parents?

11. What if an expectant mother doesn't see a family she is interested in among your clients? Do you network with other agencies and attorneys to find a good match for her?

12. Do you encourage written post-adoption contact agreements? If yes, what details do they include?

QUESTIONS TO ASK INTERNATIONAL ADOPTION AGENCIES

1. What specific countries do you work with and why were they chosen?

2. How do you determine which agencies to work with overseas and within each country?

3. What types of documentation and legal measures do you require/provide to verify that these are ethical adoptions?

4. If the child is brought to the in-country program by their family member, what is their protocol for the birth family?

5. What type of support is given to birth families in-country?

6. What type of work is done to prevent the need to place children for adoption? Are their preventative programs or other welfare programs available to help the family stay together?

7. If a child is found abandoned or abused, what is the protocol in-country?

8. What type of support is given to adoptive families throughout the process?

9. When traveling in-country, what support will be given?

10. If a law changes in the middle of our process, what is the procedure?

11. Do you provide any resources for fundraising?

12. Do you work with non-Hauge countries? If so, what does that process look like?

QUESTIONS TO ASK EMBRYO ADOPTION AGENCIES

While embryo adoption is still new, there is a growing number of agencies starting to meet the need through embryo adoption programs. However, because it is such a unique type of adoption, matching sites are also a great option.

You will find that with embryo adoption, it is much cheaper than domestic and international. With agencies, there will be fees for things like background checks and a home study, with matching sites there will be fees for your profile to stay active, but things like a home study aren't required. There are pros and cons to both, so it is helpful to explore both options so you can choose which one is right for *your* family.

Below you will find some general questions to ask for embryo adoption, as well as what you should be asking for agencies and matching sites. Many of the questions will be the same as the general questions, and most of these specific questions would be asked *after* a donor family has chosen you as the recipient family.

FOR MATCHING SITES:

1. Who runs the matching site and what are their values?

2. Does the site charge the donor families?
Note: If the answer is yes, this is a red flag. Much like with an expectant mother, there should be no fees on their end.

FOR AGENCIES:

1. Are recipient families required to adopt *all* of the donor's embryos, or is the recipient allowed to choose the quantity?

2. What fertility clinics do you work with and how are they chosen?

3. Does the recipient get to choose the IVF medical team, or is the recipient required to travel where the embryos are being stored in order to transfer?

4. How much are transfer fees?

5. Does the agency allow double donors? *(Some programs utilize egg and sperm donors to create embryos in order to create an embryo adoption program. This is up to you to decide whether or not that is something you agree with and are okay with.)*

6. Is medical testing covered and/or required?

7. Does the agency provide legal representation for both parties? Or, are both parties allowed to select their own legal representation?

AFTER SELECTING THE AGENCY OR MATCHING SITE:

1. How long have the embryos been frozen?

2. What was the freeze method? (Slow frozen or vitrified-vitrified tend to have a higher success rate.)

3. Are the embryos frozen one at a time or is there more than one to a straw? If they are frozen together, can recipient transfer one embryo and refreeze the other, or is it required they are transferred at the same time?

4. What was the mother's age at egg retrieval?

NEXT STEPS

You made it! I know this was a lot to think about and that you were asked some really personal, tough questions. But these are all things that need to be brought to light before you put pen to paper and start the adoption process. We hope to see healthier families, smoother processes, better support for families and birth families both along the way to adoption and after the fact. And unless you've got a good grasp and plan going in, that will be harder to achieve. Now that you've completed this, you may be thinking, "So now what?"

At this point, you may have realized there are some things that need to be worked through before you make any big decisions and start calling agencies, and that is a *good* thing. That is why we created this resource. I've walked with too many families who rushed into it and are paying the price now.

Whether you have some work to do or you've got your agency chosen and have started printing off that mountain of paperwork, your work as a parent is never done. You should always be learning, growing, and educating yourself. While you wait, I encourage you to head back over to the Spoonful of Jordan Shop and look through recommended reading materials, people to follow on social media, conferences and workshops to attend. The more you educate yourself before your child comes home, the better off your family will be. This will also help you with some of those trainings and continuing education hours you'll be required to do.

I hope that this has been helpful, healing, and made you feel well-equipped to walk this road. Every adoption process and story is different. It's not for the faint of heart, but it's more than worth it. Family is worth fighting for, and I can't wait to see the many ways you and your family are going to be used for a greater purpose.

AGENCY MUST-HAVES LIST

Use this as a worksheet to brainstorm and develop the close-handed, non-negotiable requirements for selecting your agency.

MY TOP 3 AGENCIES

Use the following pages to document your three favorite agencies after you have decided on your must-haves AND completed your research. You will select your agency from this list!

Use the free space below to keep an ongoing list of the agencies you want to reach out to before selecting your Top 3.

AGENCY 1 NAME:

LOCATION:

MAIN CONTACT NAME:

MAIN CONTACT'S EMAIL:

MAIN CONTACT'S PHONE:

WHAT I LIKE MOST:

CONCERNS I HAVE:

NEXT WEBINAR OR INFORMATIONAL MEETING:

AGENCY 2 NAME:

LOCATION:

MAIN CONTACT NAME:

MAIN CONTACT'S EMAIL:

MAIN CONTACT'S PHONE:

WHAT I LIKE MOST:

CONCERNS I HAVE:

NEXT WEBINAR OR INFORMATIONAL MEETING:

AGENCY 3 NAME:

LOCATION:

MAIN CONTACT NAME:

MAIN CONTACT'S EMAIL:

MAIN CONTACT'S PHONE:

WHAT I LIKE MOST:

CONCERNS I HAVE:

NEXT WEBINAR OR INFORMATIONAL MEETING:

PERSONAL NOTES

ABOUT THE AUTHOR

Christa Jordan is Texas-born and raised and earned her Bachelor's degree in Social Work from the University of North Texas in 2010. She has spent the last ten years as a social justice advocate in capacities that have ranged from serving domestic abuse survivors, mentoring foster children, and organizing match events for children waiting to be adopted.

From 2013-2015, she and her husband went through their own adoption journey, completing a private, international adoption from Japan for their son Kai. She loves movie nights with her family, cooking up tasty and healthy dishes, all things Disney, being the go-to crunchy girl of her friend group, being a non-crazy gymnastics mom, watching her dog and son chase each other, and all the good coffee and red wine and dark chocolate things.

She lives in Dallas, TX and can usually be found watching *Mary Poppins* for the hundredth time. She invites you to continue learning, join the conversation, and follow her journey at spoonfulofjordan.com or @spoonfulofjordanblog on Instagram.

51259036R00063

Made in the USA
Columbia, SC
19 February 2019